ELECTRONICS BASICS

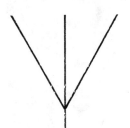

Transistors

U.S. 8c

906

Progress in Electronics

AN EARLY VERSION OF A BELL LABS 32 MICRO-
PROCESSOR ON A CHIP ON 1.5 CENTIMETERS SQUARE.

ELECTRONICS BASICS

by
Carl Laron

Illustrated by
Art Seiden

With Photographs

Created and Produced by
Arvid Knudsen

●

Prentice-Hall, Inc.
Englewood Cliffs, New Jersey

To my father.

Other **High-Tech Basics** Books in Series

COMPUTER BASICS *by Hal Hellman*
VIDEO BASICS *by J. T. Yurko*
HOME COMPUTER BASICS *by Jeffrey Rothfeder*
PHOTOGRAPHY BASICS *by Vick Owens-Knudsen*
COMPUTER PROGRAMMING BASICS *by Lawrence Stevens*
MONEY BASICS *by G. David Wallace*

Text copyright © 1984 by Carl Laron and Arvid Knudsen
Illustrations copyright © 1984 by Art Seiden

Book design by Arvid Knudsen

Printed in the United States of America   · J

Prentice-Hall International, Inc., London
Prentice-Hall of Australia, Pty. Ltd., Sydney
Prentice-Hall of Canada, Inc., Toronto
Prentice-Hall of India Private Ltd., New Delhi
Prentice-Hall of Japan, Inc., Tokyo
Prentice-Hall of Southeast Asia Pte. Ltd., Singapore
Whitehall Books Limited, Wellington, New Zealand
Editora Prentice-Hall do Brasil Ltda., Rio de Janeiro

10 9 8 7 6 5 4 3 2 1

Library of Congress Cataloging in Publication Data

Laron, Carl.
    Electronics basics.

    Includes index.
    Summary: Discusses electronics, what it means in our lives, and what the future has in store.
    1. Electronics—Juvenile literature. [1. Electronics]   I. Seiden, Art, ill.   II. Knudsen, Arvid.   III. Title.
TK7820.L3   1984   621.381   83-21308
ISBN 0-13-250143-0   (Rev.)

CONTENTS

Photo courtesy of Texas Instruments, Inc.

Preface: The Wonders of Electronics

Have you ever stopped to think about how important electronics is in your life? The easiest way to do that is with an experiment. Take a piece of paper and a pencil and make a list of everything your family owns that you think electronics plays a part in. Look around carefully and make the list as complete as you can. But before you start, let me tell you that this is a trick question.

You probably were able to get the easy ones—your radio, record player, video game or computer, electric lights, and, of course, your TV. What about some of the harder ones, like your family's car or microwave oven? Consider the pencil and paper you're holding. They aren't electronic devices, but electronic devices or machinery are used to make them. The same is true of the chair you're sitting in, your kitchen table, and just about anything else you can think of.

So you can see that without electronics, our lives would be very different. Electronic devices entertain us, help us learn, light our homes, cook our meals, warm us in the winter, cool us in the summer, and let us make things more easily, quickly, and cheaply.

We live in an age of electronic magic. But have you ever wondered about the magic behind *the magic? What exactly is electronics, what is it that makes it so special, and how did we learn of its marvels?*

The story is a wonderful one. It's about one of the tiniest things in the universe, and how it is responsible for one of the mightiest forces we know. It's also a story that's far from over. Great discoveries are still being made in laboratories all over the world.

The story is what this book is all about.

Carl Laron

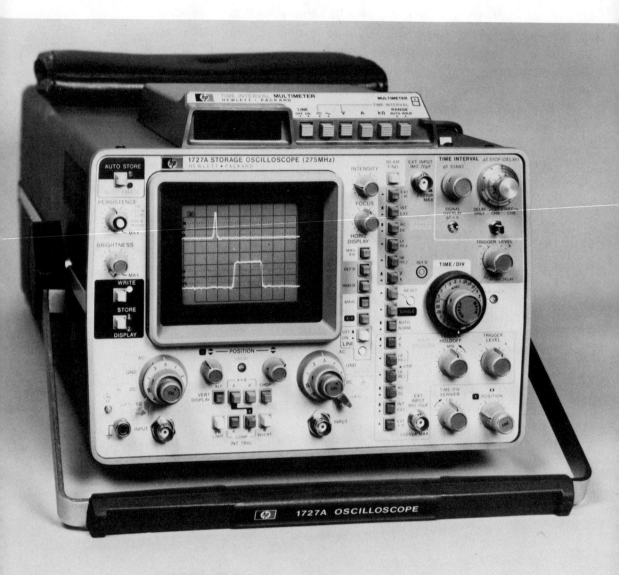

CHANGING ELECTRICAL VOLTAGES IN VISIBLE
WAVE FORMS ON IT'S CRT (TV SCREEN).

1 Matter, Atoms, Electrons, and Electricity

People have been on the planet Earth for a very long time, but we've only known about electricity for a very short time. The first important discoveries were made by the ancient Greeks. They were very fond of a certain stone. It was popular for ornaments and as a good luck charm.

It also had another property. Around the year 600 B.C., the philosopher Thales noticed that if he rubbed the stone, it would pick up small pieces of lint or straw from his clothes. We now know that magical stone as amber, but the Greeks had another name for it; they called it *elektron*. The words *electron, electronics,* and *electricity* all come from that name.

About 2,200 years later, in the year 1600, an English doctor named William Gilbert (one of his patients was none other than Queen Elizabeth I) became interested in amber's strange ability.

Gilbert also wondered if amber was the only material that could attract objects. He soon began rubbing other items, using pieces of silk and wool, and before long he had found over twenty other substances—including glass, sulphur, and various gems—that could, in his words "take hold of items and embrace them, as if with arms extended." The mysterious property, then, did not belong to amber alone. Instead, he concluded, it was a characteristic of all "matter."

But the question of what caused that property was still unanswered. The Greeks thought that amber had a "soul." Gilbert believed that "an invisible fluid" was responsible. We now know that neither of those theories was correct. To find the right answer we have to look a little more closely at the things we call matter.

ATOM

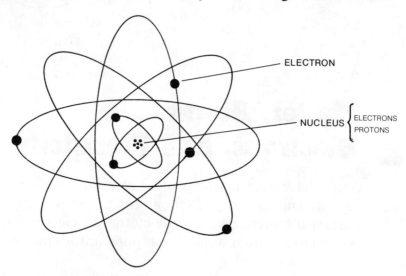

ELECTRON

NUCLEUS { ELECTRONS PROTONS

Matter and Atoms

Matter is all around us. Indeed, it *is* us. Scientifically speaking, matter is defined as anything that has weight or takes up space.

Now we know the definition of matter, but what exactly is matter, and why does it appear in so many different forms? By the early 1800s, scientists had come to the conclusion that all matter was made up of yet smaller pieces of matter called atoms. The word "atom" was taken from the Greek word *atomos*, which means "indivisible," describing something that cannot be divided.

Of course, we now know that the atom is not really indivisible. It can be broken up into yet smaller pieces, or particles, called electrons, protons, and neutrons.

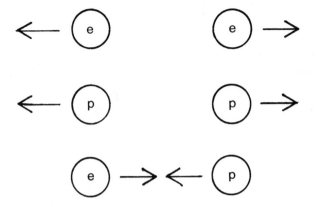

Two of those particles—the electron and the proton—have an interesting property: They are charged. What that means is that when two electrons, which carry a negative charge, are brought close together, they repel each other. The same is true for two protons, which carry a positive charge. But when a negative electron and a positive proton are brought close together, they attract each other.

We've now learned one of the most basic laws of electronics —the law of electrical charges—and by now you might be getting some inkling of why the amber, glass, and the others acted the way they did when they were rubbed. But to explain the mystery completely, we need one more piece of the puzzle.

If you look at a diagram of a simple atom—the helium atom, for instance—you will see that it is made up of a central portion, called the nucleus, and the outer electrons. The nucleus is made up of protons and neutrons. Notice that the helium atom has an equal number of protons and electrons, as does every atom.

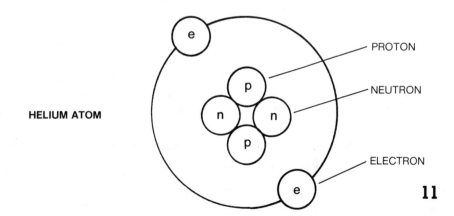

HELIUM ATOM

PROTON

NEUTRON

ELECTRON

Electrons and Electricity

But atoms don't always stay that way. The "atomic" forces holding the protons and neutrons together in the nucleus are very strong. The power of a nuclear explosion is created when the bonds holding those particles together in the nucleus are broken. But the bonds holding the electron to the nucleus are weak in some atoms. Materials made of that type of atom are called *conductors*. Thanks to the weak bonds between the electron and the nucleus, electrons can easily pass from one atom to the next in conductors.

In other atoms, the electrons are bound much more tightly. Materials made up of those atoms are called *insulators*. Because of the tight bonds between the electron and the nucleus, there is little or no movement of electrons in insulators.

But even though we call many things conductors or insulators doesn't mean that they all act the same way. Some conductors conduct better than others, while some insulators insulate better than others. It's a bit like baseball—there are a lot of teams playing the same game, but not all the teams play it as well.

Now we're ready to go back and take another look at Thales' and Gilbert's observation. As you might have guessed by now, the attracting powers were caused by electrons. Normally in nature objects have a neutral charge. That means they are neither positive nor negative, because they have an equal number of protons and electrons. But if electrons are either added to or taken away from an object, that object is said to be charged. With that in mind, let's see what happens when you rub two objects together.

In Gilbert's experiment, when the objects were rubbed with the silk or the wool, electrons were transferred between the object and the cloth. As we now know, that means that the object picked up a charge. If the object lost electrons, the charge it picked up was positive, because the object had more protons than electrons. If, on the other hand, it gained electrons, the charge that the object picked up was negative, because the object then had more electrons than protons.

Because a charged object is either more positive or negative than it should be, there is always an attraction between an uncharged object and a charged one. It doesn't matter whether the charge is positive or negative, because a positively charged object is looking for some way to replace its missing electrons, while a negatively charged one is looking for a way to get rid of its extra electrons.

We still haven't answered one question: Why don't all objects become charged when they are rubbed? Let's try another experiment to see if we can find out. Get two combs—one made of plastic, the other of metal. Make sure your hair is completely dry, then comb your hair with the plastic comb. Your comb is now charged. Like Thales' amber, it can easily pick up small bits of paper or lint. What about your hair? It too is charged. Little pieces of paper will stick to it as well.

Now try it again with the metal comb. This time neither your hair nor your comb is charged. Can you guess why? We'll give you a hint—remember what we said about insulators and conductors.

The plastic comb and your hair are insulators. When electrons are exchanged between insulators they have no place to go. That's because the insulators will not let electrons move through them. The charge sits there on the surface of the insulator until it either escapes into the air or a conductor is touched to it, letting the charge "leak" away.

Now, what about the metal comb? It too is a conductor. Your body is also a conductor, though not a very good one. Even so, no matter how fast or hard you comb your hair, charge has no chance to build up. That's because the electrons pass from the comb to your hand, then to your body, and leak into the ground faster than you could possibly comb.

But if you combed your hair with the metal comb while you were wearing a rubber glove on your hand, the comb would become charged. The reason is that the electrons no longer have a path to follow to escape into the ground. That's because the rubber glove is an insulator. By wearing the glove you would have insulated the comb from your hand.

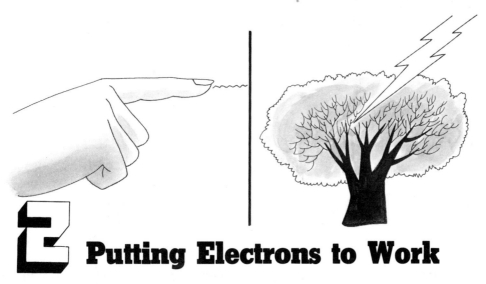

2 Putting Electrons to Work

The type of electricity we learned about in the last chapter is called *static electricity*. It's called that because it is static—it just sits there. The shock you get when you touch a piece of metal after shuffling across a woolen rug and the flash of lightning that startles you on a rainy night are both caused by static electricity.

Static electricity can also be useful. Those dry copying machines in your school and library use static electricity to make their copies. Static electricity is also used in making sandpaper and in certain methods of painting.

But most electronic devices do not use static electricity. Instead, they use electrons in motion to get the job done.

Take a look at the accompanying illustration. In it there are two charged balls. The one marked *A* is positively charged; the one marked *B* is negatively charged.

If a good conductor, such as a piece of copper wire, were connected between the two balls, the extra electrons in *B* would flow into the conductor and onto ball *A*. The electrons would keep flowing until there were an equal number of electrons in both balls.

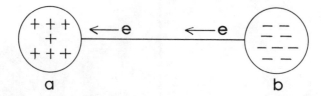

a   b

What causes that flow of electrons? Quite simply, it is the difference in charges. That difference in charges creates a pressure that forces the electrons from an area where there are too many to an area where there are not enough. That pressure is given the name of *potential*; it is also known as *voltage*. Thus, it is the voltage that causes the electrons to move through a conductor. The unit used to measure the amount of voltage is called, logically enough, the *volt*.

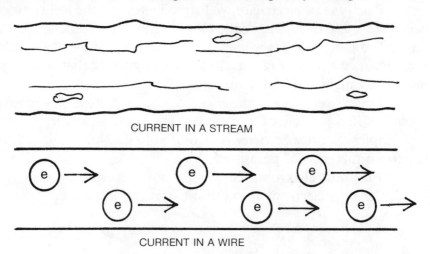

CURRENT IN A STREAM

CURRENT IN A WIRE

The flow of electrons through a conductor is called the *current*. The easiest way to keep from confusing current and voltage is to think of a conductor as a stream. The water that flows through that stream causes a current. The pressure that causes that stream to flow is the difference in elevation, or potential, between the head of a stream and its mouth.

The unit used to measure current flow is the *ampere* or amp.

There's still one more thing we have to account for. If there was a difference of potential (voltage) between balls *A* and *B*, why didn't the electrons cross from *B* to *A* before the wire was in place? The answer is that the air resists the flow of electrons through it.

But if you were to increase the voltage so that the difference in the charges was large enough, the air would not be able to hold back the electrons any longer. The electrons would jump through the air from ball to ball in the form of a spark.

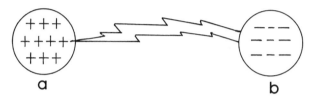

Air is not the only thing that resists the flow of electrons. But you know that already from what we said about insulators. In fact, everything, even the best conductors, resists the flow of electrons at least a little bit.

What all of this means is that for any current to flow, the voltage has to be high enough to overcome any "resistance" in its path. The unit used to measure resistance is the *ohm*.

From what we've said so far, you've probably figured out that voltage, current, and resistance are pretty closely related. In fact, if you know two of those things for a particular electronic circuit, you can easily figure out the third. The rule for doing that is called Ohm's Law:

$$E = I \times R$$

Where *E* is the voltage, *I* is the current, and *R* is the resistance of a particular circuit.

Let's try an example: A very common component in electronic circuits is the *resistor*. As you can tell from its name, its purpose is to resist the flow of electrons. Say we know that the value of a certain resistor is 5 ohms and, using a voltmeter, we measure the voltage across that resistor to be 10 volts. The current then is the voltage divided by the resistance, or $\frac{10}{5}$ = 2 amps.

We're ready now to look at our first electronic circuit. It is made up of three parts—a source of electrons (the battery), a load (in this case, a flashlight bulb), and the conductors (wires) that connect them.

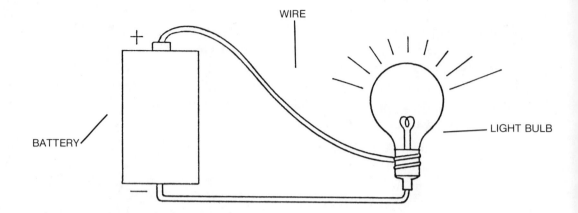

WIRE

+

BATTERY

LIGHT BULB

The Battery

The battery is a fascinating device, and there is an interesting story behind its discovery. Briefly, the first battery came about because of a feud between two great men. In 1790, Luigi Galvani noticed during the dissection of a frog that when he touched the metal scalpel to the nerve in the frog's leg, the leg twitched. Galvani became convinced that the electricity he saw was generated by the frog itself.

Alessandro Volta (as in *volt*—the unit was named in his honor) bitterly disagreed. He was convinced that it was the metal devices used in the dissection that caused the electricity. Spurred by the argument, Volta developed his Voltaic Pile. That pile was made up of a stack of alternating copper and zinc disks. In between each

GE'S NEW DESK TOP CHARGE 8 T.M.
RECHARGEABLE BATTERY CHARGER
FOR HEAVY BATTERY USERS.

18

Photo courtesy of General Electric, Inc.

disk was a piece of cardboard that had been soaked in either a solution of acid or salt in water. Using that primitive battery, Volta was able to produce a steady flow of electricity in one direction.

It's easy for you to repeat Volta's experiments. All you need do is to cut a small piece of cardboard or blotter paper and soak it in very salty water. If you then sandwich the damp paper between a penny and a nickel and connect a sensitive meter to the coins, the meter will measure a small voltage. You could make a far better battery by taking a carbon rod and a strip of zinc and placing them in a glass jar containing acid and water.

The kind of cells we've just talked about are called "wet" cells. They get their name from the fact that they use the action of a

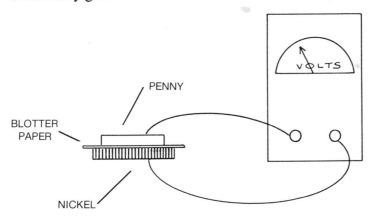

liquid on two metals to generate a voltage. The lead-acid battery in your family's car uses that type of cell. (A battery is actually a group of cells connected in series—end to end, one after the other.) Most of the other batteries that you are familiar with are "dry" cells —they use a chemical reaction between dry materials to generate a voltage.

Remember we said that the current from a battery flows only in one direction. Because of that, the voltage produced is called DC, "direct current." The voltage from your wall outlet is quite different. It is called AC, "alternating current," because the direction of the current flow changes at a very fast rate, usually 60 times per second. Your power company uses alternating current, because AC is easier to distribute over a wide area using power lines.

The Electric Light Bulb

Not long after the discovery of the battery, early electronics experimenters learned one other fact: If you pass enough current through something it will get hot. And if something gets hot enough, it will first glow and then burn.

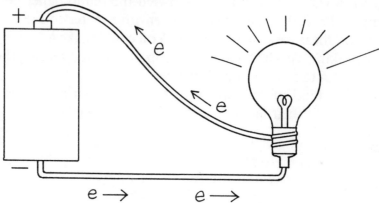

The race was then on to put that finding to practical use, or, more specifically, to invent an artificial source of light. The first to succeed was Thomas Edison. His light bulb used a carbonized thread heated by a current to the point of burning. To prevent that burning, Edison put the thread in a glass bulb from which all of the air had been removed.

Today's light bulbs don't differ all that much from Edison's design. Most bulbs are now filled with gas for safety, and metal alloy *filaments* (the wire that the current is passed through) have replaced the carbonized thread, but the basic principle is still the same.

We now have the two major parts of our circuit. But before anything happens, they have to be connected together. That's done by running a wire from the positive terminal (end) of the battery to one side of the light bulb and a second wire from the negative terminal of the battery to the other side of the light bulb. When that is done, electrons flow from the negative terminal of the battery, through the bulb, and back to the positive terminal of the battery, following the closed path. They will continue to follow the path, and flow only in the direction we've described, until either the circuit is disconnected (opened) or the battery or light bulb wears out.

BATTERY   LIGHT BULB

Before we move on, there's one last thing we should mention. When we drew the picture of the simple circuit, we showed what the battery and the light bulb looked like and all of the physical connections between the devices. That was easy for something simple, but if you try to do that for a TV, video game, or computer, you'll run into problems. Among those problems will be the fact that the drawing will be incredibly hard to follow. Instead, electronic circuits are almost always drawn in the form of *schematics*. In a schematic, instead of drawing what the device looks like, it is shown as an easily recognized symbol. Also, all of the electronic connections between the devices are shown, but they are not the same as the physical ones. In other words, a schematic diagram will let you see easily and clearly how a circuit works electronically, but not how to build it step by step.

Look at the schematic diagram for our battery/light-bulb circuit. Notice how the battery and the light bulb have been replaced by their schematic symbols.

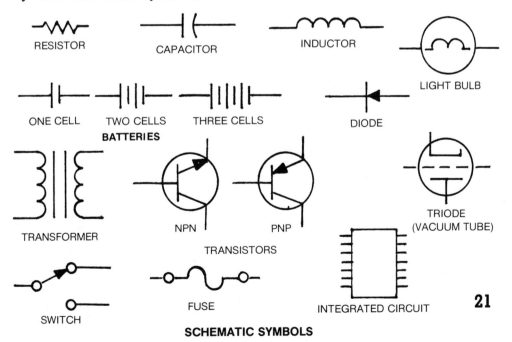

RESISTOR   CAPACITOR   INDUCTOR

LIGHT BULB

ONE CELL   TWO CELLS   THREE CELLS   DIODE
BATTERIES

TRANSFORMER   NPN   PNP   TRIODE
(VACUUM TUBE)

                    TRANSISTORS

SWITCH   FUSE   INTEGRATED CIRCUIT

SCHEMATIC SYMBOLS

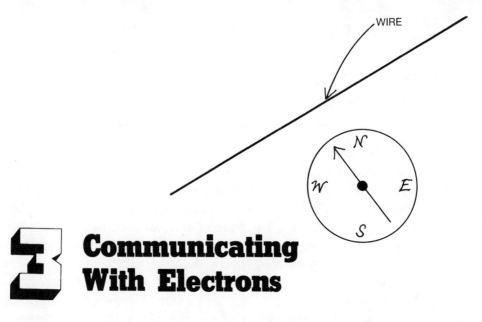

3 Communicating With Electrons

Not long after scientists began to learn about electricity, they began searching for uses for this newly found knowledge. One of the first projects that drew attention was finding some way to send speech over a long distance. Several early telegraph systems had already been tried by the end of the eighteenth century. Some used a single wire, some used as many wires as there were characters to be transmitted, but none of them worked well enough to be worthwhile.

Then, in 1819, Danish physicist Hans Christian Oersted placed a small compass near a wire that was carrying a current. His discovery that the compass needle was affected by the current in the wire proved something that had been suspected since the time of Thales and the ancient Greeks—that electricity and magnetism are closely related.

Some say that Oersted's discovery was one of the most important ever made. After all, it eventually led to such things as electromagnets, electric motors, electric power generation, and the rise of our industrial society. It also made it possible to transmit voices over long distances.

The first practical applications of electromagnetism were the telegraph and the telephone. Joseph Henry, an American scientist, opened the door to those inventions in 1830 when he showed that he could operate an electromagnet at a distance of over 1,000 feet. An

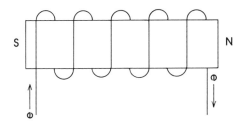

electromagnet is a coil of wire, usually wrapped around an iron core, that acts just like a very strong natural magnet when current passes through it.

From there it was only fourteen years until Samuel F. B. Morse ushered in our modern age of communications with the establishment of his Baltimore-to-Washington telegraph line. The first voice communication took place in 1876 when Alexander Graham Bell uttered his now famous "Come here, Mr. Watson. I need you."

THIS MODEL OF BELL'S FIRST TELEPHONE IS A DUPLICATE OF THE INSTRUMENT THROUGH WHICH SPEECH SOUNDS WERE FIRST TRANSMITTED ELECTRICALLY, 1875.

A MODEL OF ALEXANDER GRAHAM BELL'S ORIGINAL TELEPHONE OF 1875 IN WHICH SPEECH SOUNDS WERE FIRST TRANSMITTED ELECTRICALLY.

Two people could now communicate over longer distances than ever before, provided that there was a wire between them. But it wasn't good enough.

Wireless Communication

The discovery that electricity and magnetism are related started a lot of debate and experimentation. One of the theories proposed was that certain electrical occurrences would produce electromagnetic "waves," waves that could be created at one point and detected at another, distant, point.

In 1887 a German professor, Heinrich Hertz, proved the existence of those waves. But it was an Italian experimenter, Guglielmo Marconi, who found how to use those waves to communicate without wires, and in the process changed all our lives. By 1895 Marconi was able to transmit signals for distances of over a mile. In 1901 he succeeded in sending a wireless signal across the Atlantic. The age of global communications had begun.

Before we go any further, it is important that we understand what a wave is. Of course you've seen waves at the beach or ripples in a puddle or a pond, but to get to know waves a little better, let's try an experiment.

First, gather together a few marbles and some small pieces of cardboard. Next, fill your bathtub with water. (It's a good idea to tell your mother or father what you are doing and get their permission first.)

Once the tub is nearly full, turn off the faucet. Wait until the surface of the water is completely calm, then take one of the marbles and drop it gently into the center of the tub.

Watch what happens. A ripple forms at the point where the marble enters the water, and that ripple seems to travel away from that point in ever widening circles. That ripple is, of course, a wave.

Do you know what causes the wave to form? Well, if you could look at the wave in ultra-close-up and in ultra-slow motion, here's what you would see: When the marble hits the surface, some of the water that's in its way is forced aside. Since that water has nowhere else to go, it is pushed upward, above the original surface

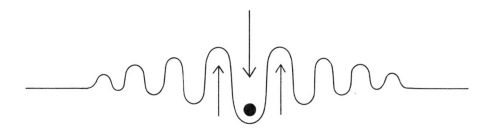

of the water. What's happening here, then, is that the force of the marble entering the water creates a circular wall of water that rises above the original surface.

The force of gravity being what it is, eventually the wall rises so high that the weight of the water in it forces it to collapse. But what happens when the wall collapses? Well, the force of the falling wall forces the water in its path aside, building up yet another circular wall. And so on, and so on, and so on.

We know that there is motion in a wave, but what is it that is actually moving? As long as we have a bathtub full of water, let's try one more experiment.

Float one of the pieces of cardboard on the surface of the water. Drop a marble gently into the tub and watch what happens to the cardboard. As the wave reaches the cardboard, the cardboard moves up and down but the wave does not carry the cardboard along with it as it passes. Try this experiment several times to convince yourself that the same thing always happens.

Now, what have we proved? Well, if the water itself was moving, the cardboard that was floating on the water would be carried along as the wave passed. Instead, it is motion caused by the falling marble, the "energy" of the falling marble, that moves through the water.

Electromagnetic waves are similar to the waves we've just looked at, but there are some important differences. For one thing, electromagnetic waves travel incredibly fast—186,000 miles per second—which is also the speed of light. For another, they can travel through air as well as through the vacuum of space. In fact, some of the most important work in modern astronomy is being done with powerful computer-controlled radio telescopes.

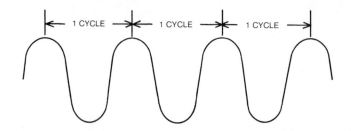

Now take a look at the accompanying drawing of an electro-magnetic wave. Notice that the pattern repeats over and over. Every complete repetition is called a *cycle*. The distance from the beginning of a cycle to its end is called the *wavelength*.

The number of times a cycle repeats in one second is called the *frequency*. Frequency is measured in *hertz*, which are cycles per second. (That's the same Hertz we mentioned earlier; most of the great men in electronics history have been honored by having a unit named after them.) When you hear your favorite radio station identify its location on the dial with a number, that number is the frequency of its carrier; the *carrier* is the electromagnetic wave that "carries" the information you hear.

If it is an AM station, the frequency is given in kilohertz (thousands of hertz); if it is an FM station, the frequency is given in megahertz (millions of hertz).

Speaking of AM and FM, have you ever wondered what those initials stand for? They refer to the way that information is transmitted. A carrier wave can't communicate voices and music—it is just a steady signal. To make voice and music communication possible, the transmitter mixes, or combines, the carrier with another wave that's much lower in frequency. Information is encoded onto that second wave in one of two ways. If it is "amplitude modulated" —that's AM—information is transmitted by varying the height (the amplitude) of the second wave. If it is "frequency modulated"— that's FM—the frequency of the second wave is varied.

Television

Our discussion of the ways we use electronics to communicate would not be complete without at least some mention of the glowing one-eyed monster—television—that's such an important part of our lives.

A television broadcasting and receiving system is far more complicated than a radio system, but the basics are the same. Two carriers are involved: One is for the audio (sound) and the other is for the video (picture).

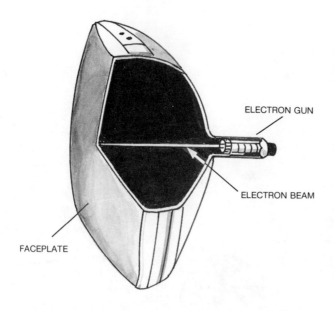

ELECTRON GUN

ELECTRON BEAM

FACEPLATE

The video information is used to generate the picture you see on the TV screen. That TV screen is actually the business end of something called a *cathode ray tube*, or CRT for short.

A CRT is shaped more or less like a funnel. At the wide end is the screen that you see. The inside of the screen is coated with a phosphor—a substance that glows when it is struck by an electron. A black-and-white CRT uses a phosphor that glows white; color pictures are made using red, blue, and green phosphors arranged in a tight pattern, or *matrix*.

At the narrow end of the tube is an *electron gun*. The purpose of that gun is to shoot a steady stream of electrons at the screen.

Of course, if there were no order to the way that the electrons struck the screen, all we would get is a pretty glow. Nice, but not terribly exciting to watch. Instead, the beam of electrons is swept across the screen in a series of lines starting at the upper right-hand corner and ending in the lower left-hand corner of the screen.

What's happening, then, is that the image you see is being laid down in a series of lines, 525 of them, not as a single picture. But because the whole process is very fast—your TV traces out 15,750 of those lines every second—your eye can't tell the difference.

COLOR PICTURES ARE MADE USING (R) RED, (B) BLUE, AND (G) GREEN PHOSPHORS AR-RANGED IN A TIGHT PATTERN, OR MATRIX. IF WE PUT A MAGNIFYING GLASS TO THE CRT (SCREEN)—THIS IS HOW CLOSE THE PHOS-PHORS WOULD APPEAR.

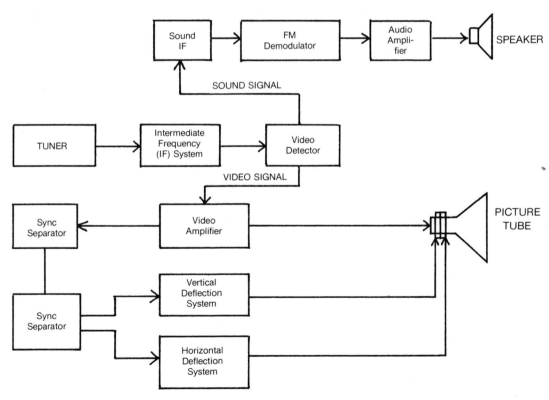

AS YOU CAN SEE FROM THIS BLOCK DIAGRAM, A TV SET IS AN INCREDIBLY COMPLICATED DEVICE.

From Tubes to Integrated Circuits

One of the most puzzling mysteries facing those who were trying to develop an electric light bulb was why the insides of those bulbs would blacken after only a short time. We now know that the blackening was caused by high-energy electrons being flung off the filament.

In 1883, five years before Hertz's experiments and fifteen years before the discovery of the electron, Thomas Edison was trying to perfect his electric light bulb. During one of his experiments, he sealed a wire in the glass bulb, locating it near the filament but not touching it. Testing this setup, he found that when he put a positive charge on the extra wire, a small current would flow to it, away from the hot filament. When a negative charge was put on the wire, no current would flow.

Although he patented his "Edison effect," it did not solve the problem he was having with the light bulb, and he soon moved on to other things.

But the Edison effect was not forgotten. One of radio's major problems during its first decade was the lack of a good detector. A *detector* is the section of a radio receiver that, logically enough, detects the presence of the transmitted electromagnetic waves. Even the best of the early detectors was insensitive, making it difficult to communicate over long distances.

150,000 TRANSISTORS ARE CONTAINED IN THIS MICROPROCESSOR WHICH IS FOUR-TENTHS OF A SQUARE INCH. ITS CIRCUITRY IS SHOWN ON A 20-BY-20-FOOT COMPUTER PRINTOUT.

Photo courtesy of Bell Telephone Laboratories, Inc.

The need for a good detector was solved by Lee de Forest's Audion. That device, a vacuum tube whose operation was based on the Edison effect, was far better than anything else available. But it also had another interesting feature: It could take a weak signal and *amplify* it, that is, make it much stronger.

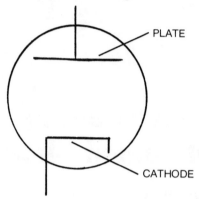

What is a vacuum tube? Take a look at the schematic symbol for one. Notice that there are two parts to it. The part labeled "cathode" is like the filament in Edison's light bulb. It is what emits the electrons. The part labeled "plate" is like the wire in Edison's experiments. If it is made positive, electrons flow to it from the cathode. But if it is made negative, no electrons flow. A two-element tube like this one is called a *diode*.

Now let's place a third element between the plate and the cathode of the tube. That element is called a *grid*. The grid is de Forest's contribution to the tube.

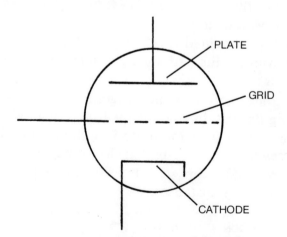

The purpose of the grid is to control how many electrons actually reach the plate. That's done by varying the voltage that is applied to the grid. (The source of that varying voltage could be a radio signal or the output of a microphone.) If the voltage to the grid is negative, the grid repels the electrons (which are also negative) back toward the cathode; but very few reach the plate. If the voltage to the grid is positive, the grid actually pulls even more electrons from the cathode to the plate. It is the grid that gives the vacuum tube the ability to amplify. A simple tube-type audio amplifier is shown in the diagram.

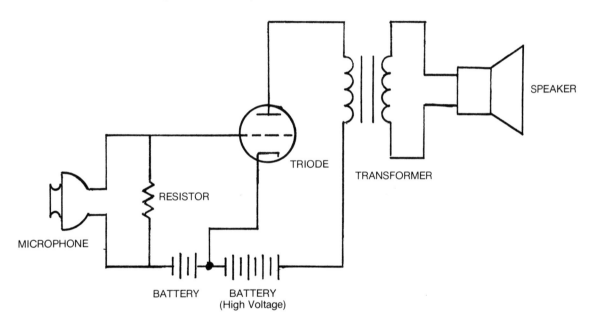

A tube with a single grid is called a *triode*. There are also tubes with two and three grids. They are called *tetrodes* and *pentodes*.

A Better Way

These days, though, the only place you are likely to find tubes is in an antique. That's because of a device invented by three scientists: William Shockley, J. Bardeen, and W. H. Brattain, who were working for Bell Laboratories. The device we're talking about is, of course, the transistor.

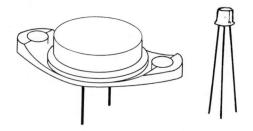

It is not surprising that Bell scientists were the ones to come up with the breakthrough—the telephone company stood to gain the most if a replacement for the vacuum tube could be found. Let's see why.

Remember what we said about resistance? Everything resists the flow of electrons, even an excellent conductor like a telephone cable. In fact, unless some type of amplifier is used to boost the signal every few miles, the resistance of the wire will cause the signal to be lost.

Up until the 1940s, the only practical device to use in an amplifier was a vacuum tube. But as good an amplifier as the vacuum tube is, it is far from perfect. Among other things, it gets hot and uses a lot of power. It also has a habit of failing when least expected. That means that maintaining tube amplifiers can be expensive, especially when you consider how many of those amplifiers are involved in something as large as our nation's phone system. The invention of the transistor in 1948 made all of those problems a thing of the past.

The transistor is possible because of a special type of material called a *semiconductor*. To understand what a semiconductor is, we have to go back a bit to our discussion of conductors. We said then that things could be considered to be either conductors or insulators. There is, in fact, a third group—that is where the semiconductors fit in. A semiconductor is an insulator that has been altered so that it conducts.

To make a semiconductor, germanium or silicon (used most often today) is changed by adding small amounts of another element such as arsenic, phosphorus, galium, or aluminum. The process of adding that element is called *doping*.

When silicon is doped, one of two things happens. Either the silicon picks up extra electrons or it doesn't have enough—it depends on the material used in the doping. Silicon with too many electrons is called an *n-type semiconductor*. Silicon with too few electrons is called a *p-type semiconductor*. And the absence of an electron is called a *hole*. When those holes move through the semiconductor, the effect is the same as a moving positive charge.

Semiconductors can be used to make devices that behave like vacuum tubes, but without the problems of vacuum tubes.

A semiconductor diode is made by putting an n-type and a p-type semiconductor together. This diode acts just like the tube diode we talked about before in that it will pass current in one direction only.

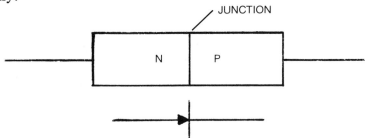

The transistor is the equivalent of the tube triode. It is made by sandwiching a very thin piece of one type of semiconductor material between two pieces of the opposite type of material.

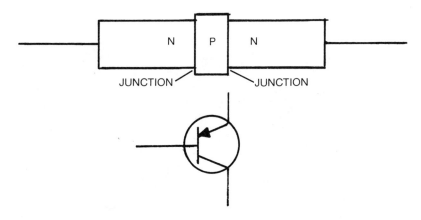

Photo courtesy of Apple Computer Corp.

Integrated Circuits: The Tiniest Marvel

Transistors are made by doping small areas of a larger silicon wafer—a very thin slice of silicon. It wasn't very long after the development of the transistor that researchers got the idea to put more than one transistor on a wafer.

The first *integrated circuit*, or IC, was demonstrated in 1959. It was a *flip-flop*—a logic circuit used in computers. All of the transistors, resistors, capacitors, and interconnections were made completely out of a single piece of germanium.

We've come a long way from that first four-transistor IC. For instance, the MC68000, a computer microprocessor and the heart of such machines as Apple's Lisa, contains 68,000 transistors, as well as resistors, capacitors, and other components. That many transistors is typical for that type of IC. But an IC could contain many more components.

Once, a computer's circuitry filled a room. Today, it is possible to put all that circuitry on a piece of silicon that's smaller than a dime. What will tomorrow bring?

The World of Tomorrow

We live in a world full of electronic wonders. Inventions and developments that were pure science fiction when your parents were your age are now taken for granted. But what of the future? What kind of wonders can your children look forward to?

Computers

To say that computers have exploded onto the scene these past few years would be an understatement. The reason, of course, is cost. Thanks to IC technology, computers that cost thousands of dollars only a few years ago now can be bought for less than $100. What's more, if you held them in your lap, they probably would not even crease your pants.

Microprocessors, the parts of the computer that "compute," are starting to show up everywhere and anywhere. Consider this, for instance: If your family just bought a new car, the odds are good that it contains one or more of those devices. Among other things, car makers are using microprocessors in the ignition system, in the instrument system, in the heating/air-conditioning system, and to tell you if something—including one of the other microprocessors—is not working properly.

Photo courtesy of NCR

But as good as our modern computers are, they are headed for a dead end. The reason is that they are still nothing more than complex adding machines—they can answer a question only if they are provided with all the information that they need. If some of the information is missing, or if it has to make a decision that is outside of its programming, the computer is helpless. It cannot reason out a problem the way a person can.

That may not be the case for long. Several of the world's most powerful computer companies have joined with the Japanese government in a project to develop a computer that can think like a person. If they succeed, it could be the most important invention since the wheel.

Video

Next to the computer, the consumer electronics field that has grown the most in the last few years is video.

By the time you read this book, pocket and wristwatch televisions—much like the fanciful gadgets used by Dick Tracy of the comics—will be commonplace. From what we now know of IC's, getting the circuitry down to a small size was not the main problem in developing such a gadget. Instead, it was what to do with the CRT.

The answer turns out to be to get rid of it. Instead of a CRT, a *liquid crystal display* (LCD) is used—the same kind of LCD that's used in your watch and calculator.

Work on large-scale LCD's and other types of flat-panel displays is continuing. If that work pays off, the TV display of the future could measure 10 feet across by a quarter-inch thick and hang on your wall like a picture.

Another exciting development is digital TV. In digital TV, the video information that is received by the TV set is *digitized*; that is, it is converted into a string of 0's and 1's just like computer data.

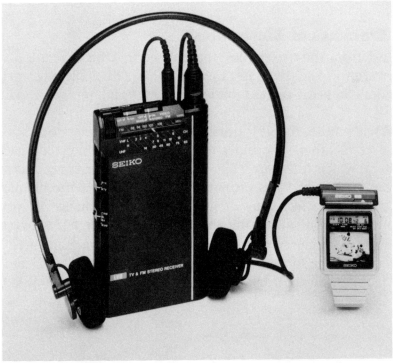

41

Photo courtesy of Seiko Corp.

The advantage is that once the video information is converted into something resembling computer data, it can be treated like computer data. For instance, it can be stored in a computer memory and played back later, just like a videotape. Also, special effects such as slow motion, fast motion, and variable zoom (close up) are easily within the capabilities of a digital TV system.

Other things to look forward to are *high-definition TV*, where the picture quality will be as good as that of a photographic slide, and *three-dimensional TV*. Various companies are hard at work on both types of systems.

Other Branches of Electronics

Just from these examples you can see that we have a lot to look forward to. And that's just the beginning. Other exciting work is being done in areas such as audio, microwaves, lasers, and solar power.

What's more, things learned in one branch of electronics are finding uses in others. Consider digital audio. The new compact disk system, which some say will eventually put ordinary records in the same antique category as vacuum tubes, uses computer techniques to create a near-perfect copy of the original performance. If you close your eyes, you will not be able to tell the difference between the original performance and the recording. And a phonograph needle will never touch the surface of these digital disks. Instead, a laser is used to pick up the recorded message without touching the disk.

Electronics and You

We've answered a lot of questions so far, but there's one left: What is your place in the world of electronics? Where do you fit in? The answer is: Anywhere you want to. One of the great things about electronics is that it offers something for just about everybody.

There are many wonderful careers that deal with electronics. For instance, if you are good in math and science and you like solving problems, then you might be interested in a career as an electrical engineer. Engineers are the ones who design the sophisticated circuits and devices that make our world what it is. Look around you: your family's TV, microwave oven, video game, and just about any other electronic device started out as an engineer's design.

If, on the other hand, you're the type of person who likes to take things apart and put them back together, maybe you would be interested in becoming a service technician. They are the people responsible for finding out why a piece of electronic equipment has stopped working and for making it work again.

Other careers in electronics include research scientist, broadcast engineer, draftsman, computer operator, computer engineer, technical writer or illustrator, electrician, engineering assistant, laboratory technician—and the list goes on and on.

Even if you don't want to make electronics your career, it can still be a fascinating hobby. Millions of people of all ages and from all around the world spend their spare time operating amateur radio stations, fixing old radios and TVs, and building circuits and projects of every description.

The true wonder of electronics, then, is that we are not limited to enjoying the products it makes possible. Instead, the wonder lies in the fact that we can help shape the world of tomorrow.

GLOSSARY

AC: Alternating current. Current that periodically changes direction.

AM: Amplitude modulation. In radio, the method of encoding information on a wave by changing its height.

Ampere: The unit of current flow named in honor of French physicist Andre Marie Ampere.

Atom: From the Greek word for indivisible, "atomos," it is the smallest piece that an element can be broken down into without losing its characteristics.

Battery: A group of cells connected one after the other.

Cathode: A negatively charged terminal.

Cell: A device that uses a chemical reaction to produce a voltage.

Charge: An excess of electrons or protons.

Circuit: A closed loop through which electrons flow.

Conductor: A material that does not oppose the flow of electrons.

CRT: Cathode ray tube; your television's picture tube is a CRT.

Current: The flow of electrons.

Cycle: A complete repetition. When talking about waves, a cycle would span from the peak of one wave to the peak of the next.

DC: Direct current. Current that always flows in the same direction.

Diode: A device made up of a slab of p-type and a slab of n-type semiconductor material. Also a two-terminal vacuum tube.

Electromagnet: An artificial magnet made by wrapping a current-carrying wire around an iron rod.

Electron: A negatively charged particle. One of the three parts of an atom.

FM: Frequency modulation. In radio, the method of encoding information on a wave by changing its frequency.

Frequency: The number of times something repeats in a period of time.

Hertz: The unit of frequency, defined as cycles-per-second and named after Heinrich Hertz.

Insulator: A material that opposes the flow of electrons.

Integrated circuit: A slab of semiconductor material with many interconnected electronic components.

Junction: The point or area where two opposite types of semiconductors are in contact.

Microprocessor: A central processing unit, or CPU, contained on a single integrated circuit. The CPU is the part of the computer that does the actual computing.

Microwave: An electromagnetic wave with an extremely short wavelength.

Neutron: One of the three particles that make up an atom, it carries no charge.

Ohm: The unit of resistance named in honor of Georg S. Ohm of Germany.

Ohm's Law: A simple formula derived by Ohm that defines the relationship between resistance, current, and voltage. It states that current is equal to voltage divided by resistance.

Plate: A positively charged terminal.

Proton: One of the three particles of an atom, it carries a positive charge.

Resistance: The opposition a material presents to the flow of electrons.

Resistor: An electronic component that resists the flow of electrons.

Semiconductor: An insulator that has been changed so that it now conducts. There are two types of semiconductor material: p-type, which is positively charged, and n-type, which is negatively charged.

Transistor: A device made by sandwiching a thin slab of one type of semiconductor material between two pieces of the opposite type.

Triode: A three-element vacuum tube.

Voltage: The difference in charge between two points. The unit of voltage is the volt, which is named in honor of Alessandro Volta.

Wave: The movement of energy from one point to another.

Wavelength: The distance between the beginning and end of a cycle.

INDEX